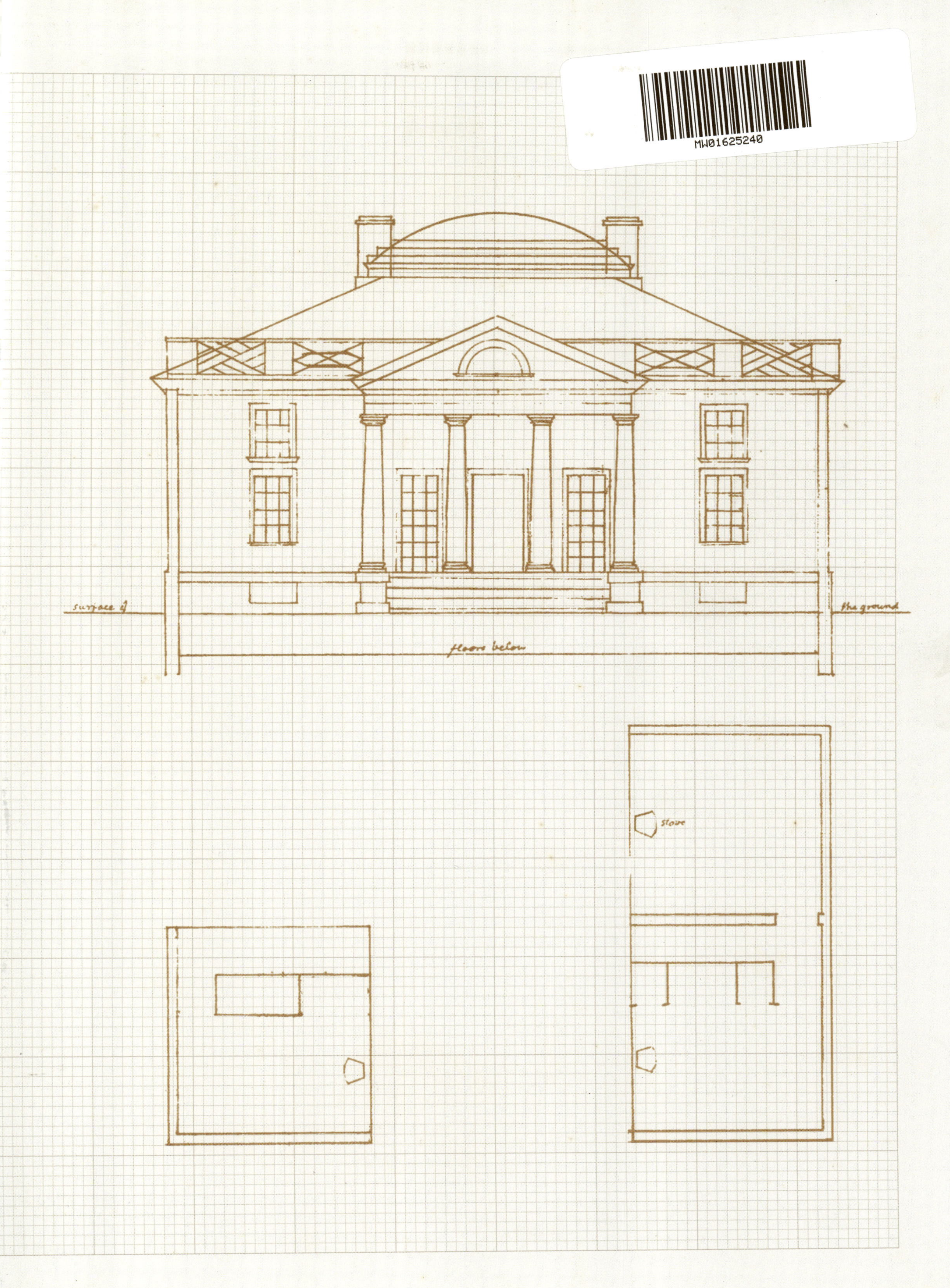
surface of
the ground
floors below
stove

BARBOURSVILLE VINEYARDS

BARBOURSVILLE VINEYARDS

TEXT AND ORIGINAL PHOTOGRAPHY BY
CHILES T. A. LARSON

BARBOURSVILLE, VIRGINIA

 Published 2008
16 15 14 13 12 11 10 09 08 1 2 3 4 5 6 7 8 9 10

Printed in Singapore

ISBN-10: 0-9818340-0-0
ISBN-13: 978-0-9818340-0-9

Book design:
Studio Mellano, Turin, Italy
Calligraphy by Chen Li

Barboursville Vineyards
17655 Winery Road
P. O. Box 136
Barboursville, Virginia 22923
www.Barboursvillewine.com

Endsheets:
Thomas Jefferson designed a number of homes for friends, but, in this 1817 architectural rendering of Barboursville, he incorporated many features that are reminiscent of Monticello.

Frontispiece:
An early morning haze shrouds the twin buildings housing the diminutive 1804 Inn, while a small herd of cows reflect the continuance of farming operations that have remained in place since James Barbour's day.

Page vi:
Thomas Jefferson designed this pavilion on the eastern edge of his vegetable garden to provide a sweeping, panoramic view of his vineyard, orchard, and beyond, as well as a place for quite reflection and contemplation.

Page ix:
The last rays of a fading afternoon sun bathe the stark brick shell of what was the imposing home of James and Lucy Barbour.

To my Great Aunt Carrie, Mrs. Robert Strode Barbour, of Green's Folly, Halifax County, Virginia. While I was a young boy she sent me books and poems, that maybe, unbeknownst to her, helped place me on a literary path.

FOREWORD

Few human endeavors are as old as the making of wine. Although poet John Milton wrote that wine grapes grew in the Garden of Eden, archaeologists trace the earliest grape fermentation to Armenia, which then spread to the Fertile Crescent and ancient Egypt. Both the Bible and the Koran are replete with references to wine. Over the next several millennia, the fruit of the vine made its way to other regions of the world, including the Western Hemisphere. Christopher Columbus brought grape cuttings with him on his second voyage to the New World. Catholic priests introduced the vine to California before 1600 and produced small quantities of ceremonial wine.

A few years later, the English introduced wine to their first permanent settlement in the Western Hemisphere when the early Jamestown settlers made wine from wild grapes. Attempts over the next two centuries to introduce European grapes to Virginia, however, met with failure. Thomas Jefferson was convinced that the region surrounding his beloved Monticello was well suited for wine production, and tried numerous times to grow European grapes. "We could, in the United States," he noted, "make as great a variety of wines as are made in Europe, not exactly of the same kinds, but doubtless as good." Despite his best efforts, Jefferson was no more successful than so many others who had tried before him. Hot, humid summers, cold winters, and a host of plant diseases and insect enemies conspired to keep European varieties from taking solid root in Virginia.

Not until growers in the nineteenth century understood the need to develop hybrids between native American and European varieties did wine making begin to succeed in Virginia. But just as grapes began to flourish in Virginia soil, the Civil War swept across the Old Dominion, destroying much in its path, including the nascent wine industry. After the war, the new state of California, unscarred by the war, and blessed with a near perfect grape-growing climate, began to dominate the American market. Virginia growers tried to recover in the first half of the twentieth century, but fought a losing battle against Prohibition, the Great Depression, and the disruptions of World War II. By the 1960s, Virginia no longer had a wine industry to speak of.

Within two decades, however, improved scientific methods applied to grape cultivation and a loosening of legal restrictions on the production and distribution of wine resulted in a remarkable comeback for the industry. By the turn of the twenty-first century, Virginia could claim some 100 wineries that produced more than 6,000 tons of grapes annually.

One of the most successful of those wineries, Barboursville Vineyards, is nestled in Orange County within sight of the ancient Blue Ridge Mountains. Spread out over more than 800 acres of rolling land owned by the Zonin family of Italy, it is also the site of the ruins of the home of Governor James Barbour. Designed by his friend Thomas Jefferson, it was regarded as the largest and finest residence in the region. Luca Paschina, general manager and master winemaker of Barboursville Vineyards, sees a direct connection between this historic property and the Sage of Monticello. "Jefferson understood better than anyone that wine gives us a sense of connection with the land," argues Paschina.

It is, therefore, only fitting that as the oldest permanent English settlement in the Western Hemisphere marks its 400th anniversary, that wine making and the rich history and stunning beauty of Barboursville Vineyards be appropriately chronicled in both word and image by one of Virginia's most respected photojournalists, Chiles T. A. Larson. For more than five decades, he has studied Virginia's past by exploring and photographing its present.

His vivid, often poignant, photographic images have graced the pages of numerous publications and have hung in the galleries of major museums, including the Virginia Historical Society. As any good winemaker knows, good wines are the result of a combination of factors - the right climate and soil, the grape itself, and the skill of the vintner. Just like fine wine, *Barboursville Vineyards: Crafting Great Wines Inspired by Spirits of the Past*, is a combination of factors - an interesting story, compellingly told in picture and word by a skilled artisan. Lovers of wine and Virginia will enjoy this book as much as they would a glass of the finest Chardonnay and Cabernet.

Charles F. Bryan, Jr.
President and CEO, Virginia Historical Society

Detail from an 1807 survey by James Madison, president of the College of William and Mary and cousin to the president of the same name, indicating the close proximity between Monticello, Montpelier (shown as "Madison's" on the map), and Barboursville (shown as "Barbour").

PREFACE

As I recall, the first time I saw the ruins of Barboursville was in the 1960s. An uncle, Charles "Mike" Houston, a well-known, veteran newspaperman with the *Richmond News Leader*, had recently purchased a weekend home within the small community of Barboursville. He had started a column, "Sidelights," which he wrote three times a week. Each Tuesday, with the dateline Barboursville, he wrote about his weekend puttering about his two-acre property, which bordered onto Sop Skillet Road. Interestingly, this little white frame house is now the home of viticulturist Fernando Franco, the current farm manager for Barboursville Vineyards.

The impression I had of this once-grand manor and of the great fire that destroyed it has not changed over the ensuing years. I learned that the house had been designed by Thomas Jefferson for James Barbour, who once served as governor of Virginia.

Although I had made several trips to the property since it was turned into Barboursville Vineyards, it was not until early September 2005, while visiting with my wife that I met Luca Paschina, the general manager and winemaker. I thought that with the success the vineyard was experiencing, there might be a good magazine feature story here to pursue. Luca, who had seen a copy of my book, *Virginia's Past Today*, surprised me by asking if I would be interested in doing a book on Barboursville.

Although flattered, I expressed some reservations on how well a book on this subject might sell. When I learned more about the accomplishments of James Barbour, together with his connection with Thomas Jefferson and of the contributions of the multi-talented Philip Mazzei, and how the Zonin family from Italy became involved with the estate some three decades earlier, I began to see the possibilities. The clincher was when Luca told me that well over 80,000 visitors tour the winery each year and that many were interested in having a book relating to these extraordinary individuals and their contributions to what is happening at Barboursville today.

The disparity of resource materials on James Barbour and Philip Mazzei are in sharp contrast to what we know and can know about Thomas Jefferson. Yet, occasional nuggets would turn up from various sources to cast a flash of insight into the makeup of these two remarkable but little-known men of the Jeffersonian period.

In 1975, the American Institute of Italian Studies published *Philip Mazzei: Jefferson's Zealous Whig*, by Sister Margherita Marchione. She writes, "It is believed that Thomas

Jefferson, a close friend of Mazzei's, gave him a copy of the original draft of the Declaration of Independence. John F. Kennedy once wrote that Mazzei had exerted significant influence on Jefferson, who paraphrased some of his writings in the Declaration."

On page 418 of the August 1881 issue of *Harper's New Monthly Magazine*, I found a couple of anecdotes illustrating what several contemporaries thought of James Barbour as a speaker. When the eccentric and caustic John Randolph of Roanoke was asked what he thought of one of Governor Barbour's eloquent and impressive speeches in Congress he said, "He clothed a beggarly idea in imperial purple, and called down the thunder of heaven to kill a gnat upon a bull's horn."

A second comment in the same issue of *Harper's New Monthly Magazine* came from a "plain countryman" on a court day in Orange County when retired President Madison and Governor Barbour addressed their neighbors and friends from the courthouse steps on the important questions of the day. "Both were eloquent, both instructive. The difference in their style of speaking was strikingly depicted by the local plain countryman." He was asked which was the greater man. Madison or Barbour. He replied, "Barbour". When asked the reason, he said, "Barbour is so great a man that I did not understand a word he said. I understood every word Madison said, and he did not tell me anything I did not know before."

As a writer and photojournalist, with a strong interest in Virginia history, I have learned there is an almost bottomless source for material here in the Old Dominion that is both visually compelling to my camera and intellectually compelling to my writing. Once when I spoke with one of my writer friends about the old adage, "A picture is worth ten thousand words," I recall he responded: "Yes, but remember it takes words to say that."

With that thought in mind, I have endeavored to bring both the images and the words as close together as possible in relating the fascinating, unfolding story that is Barboursville. In tandem with these words and images are the contributions of others in bringing together the book you hold in your hand.

My thanks to Jason W. Tesauro, who has brought together a concluding essay covering all aspects regarding the winery operations, the cuisine of Palladio Restaurant, the newly opened barrel-aging room and wine museum, and the elegant 1804 Inn and Vineyard Cottage, dating from the eighteenth century.

I also wish to thank Charles F. Bryan, Jr., for his generous introduction. During his tenure as president and chief executive officer, the Virginia Historical Society has greatly expanded its space for displaying its outstanding collections and special exhibitions.

For several years I have been a volunteer with Colonial Williamsburg's photographic services unit. The staff is outstanding and has helped me in numerous ways to keep current with expanding technical developments. I particularly want to thank lab manager Tom Austin and Barbara Lombardi for their generous spirit and patience in this regard.

There is a rendering in the book of a painting of Philip Mazzei by the French artist, Jacques-Louis David, which hangs in the Louvre in Paris. It was through the efforts of Renée Pélissier, a longtime Parisian friend, that I was able to obtain a high resolution CD of this wonderful painting. *Merci beaucoup*, Renée. Another example of international assistance comes from Federico Bonucci, who serves as a guardian of the Cathedral Square in Pisa. We met him at the Monumental Cemetery while looking in vain for the grave of Filippo Mazzei. A number of months later he located it in the little church of the Cimitero Suburbano just outside of Pisa. He sent several photographs depicting Mazzei's grave and the memorials to this outstanding patriot. Molte grazie, Federico, for your resolve.

A part of my work on this project required visiting the Zonin headquarters in Northern Italy in the small community of Gambellara, just outside Vicenza, and to their principal winery estate, the Castello d'Albola, located in Radda, in the Chianti region of Tuscany. My wife joins me in expressing our appreciation to those members of the Zonin family and staff for their warm and generous hospitality extended to us during our stay.

Not to be overlooked is my gratitude to Luca Paschina for his confidence in me to do this book, and to the outstanding staff at Barboursville for their assistance when it was needed. Also my thanks go to Joe Rountree for bringing his expertise in publishing to the project.

Finally, I wish to thank Bernice, my wife, whose many years of experience as a wine enthusiast helped in countless ways. She has been honored for her interest by being tapped for membership into two renown wine societies, the *Confrérie des Chevaliers du Tastevin* and the *Entonneurs Rabelaisiennes de Chinon*. In addition to her knowledge of wine, she is conversant in several languages and adept as an editor – a combination of skills that played such an important role in the success of this project.

BARBOURSVILLE VINEYARDS

Crafting Great Wines Inspired by Spirits of the Past

". . . we can drink wine here as cheap as we do grog,
and who will not prefer it?
Its extended use will carry health and comfort
to a much enlarged circle."

Thomas Jefferson to Monsieur de Novelly
December 13, 1818

Gazing upward at the imposing brick walls, the soaring columns of the twin porticos, and the four symmetrically matching chimneys, the eye takes in all that remains of Barboursville after a devastating fire on Christmas Day in 1884. Peering in through the entrance hall into the two-story octagonal drawing room, a visitor can readily recognize the hand of Thomas Jefferson, who designed the building for his friend and neighbor, James Barbour.

Studying these majestic ruins in the early first light of morning or during the fading twilight is to experience an uncommon quality that surrounds and links us to this special place. One can but wonder at the events that took place here in the days of Jefferson, Madison, Monroe, and scores of other notable neighbors and leaders who visited as guests of James and Lucy Barbour during the formative years of the United States.

Now a flourishing vineyard, Barboursville is a visual reminder of an earlier vital farming operation. Barbour, Jefferson, and an Italian émigré named Filippo (Philip) Mazzei all shared a vision of bringing forth a more productive use of the land through innovative farming, by introducing improved varieties of plants, vines, and trees, in addition to seeking ways of retaining soil fertility. With the passing of two centuries this vision has been fully realized.

Opposite:
Crimson dogwood leaves frame the soaring columns of Barboursville's south portico.

James Barbour: A Man of Many Achievements

Not a great deal is known about Barbour, a self-educated man of impressive talents, largely because he has been overshadowed by other statesmen, including four U. S. presidents, who were born or lived within a few miles of his plantation. Yet Barbour's spirit can be felt on the wind, passing over rows upon rows of European vinifera grapevines spreading out over 152 acres where fields of waving wheat were once successfully produced along with a number of excellent grain crops. In his day Barbour's farming operation was considered one of the most productive in Virginia.

Fields of waving wheat and other grains were once successfully produced where now row upon rows of ripening vinifera grapevines form an impression of relentless ocean waves shoreward bound.

But what of James Barbour? Who was he and what did he do during his time and place? His sparse headstone marking his final resting place, located nearby in the family burial grounds, offers scant clues. It simply spells out his name, service as a private in the 39th Virginia Militia, War of 1812, and the date of his death, June 7, 1842. This brief summation is all he had charged his son to place on his headstone. Years later, the family, finding such brevity insufficient, placed a bronze plaque on the wall behind his headstone, addressing his many achievements.

James Barbour served as governor of Virginia during the War of 1812. During his tenure, he became the first man to live in the Governor's Mansion. As a tribute to their service, portraits of former governors hang in the Virginia State Capitol. This circa 1822 portrait of Barbour, attributed to Chester Harding, hangs in the Governor's Mansion.

"I Have Rarely Known a Wiser Man"

No finer eulogy could be given than the comments expressed by President John Quincy Adams upon the death of his former cabinet member: "I have been connected with this government in one way or another, almost from its foundation to the present hour. I have known personally nearly all the great men who have been connected with its administration, and I can safely say that I have rarely known a wiser man, and never a better man, than James Barbour."

Barbour's birth, June 10, 1775, coincided with the nativity of American independence. Born into prosperous surroundings, his father, Thomas Barbour, was a well-to-do planter and leading citizen in Orange County, Virginia, who over time served as a gentleman justice, county sheriff, militia colonel, and member of the House of Burgesses. Although James had all of the social advantages that accompanied this status, by the time many of his contemporaries were setting off to the College of William and Mary and other like institutions, his father's financial fortunes had fallen into decline. As a consequence, young Barbour had to study the classics, history, and government alone at home.

Below, left: This charming cast iron gate ornament adorns the entry into the Barbour family graveyard located on the property.

Below, center: Barbour charged his son with listing only his name, military service, and the date of his death on his sparse headstone. Years later, the family, finding such brevity insufficient, placed a bronze plaque on the wall behind his headstone, addressing his many achievements.

Below, right: Three of the Barbour's four children would not reach adulthood. A poignant epitaph silently expresses the family's heartache over the loss of two of their children.

When he reached sixteen, Barbour became interested in the law. Following a course taken by many young Virginians, he first served as an assistant in a clerk's office while continuing to read the few law textbooks available to him. He then read law for a short period under a lawyer in Richmond before continuing further study on his own. Within a year of this undertaking, he put his scholarship to the practical test by serving as deputy sheriff in Orange County. In September 1793, Barbour had met all the requirements to obtain a license from the Virginia General Court to practice law throughout the Commonwealth.

Over the next several years Barbour gained in experience and in his friendship with other members of the bar, many of whom would attain distinction in the decades ahead. Two of his closest companions during the years he was riding circuit were William Wirt, who later served as attorney general in John Quincy Adams's cabinet, and Dabney Carr, Jefferson's nephew.

Barbour Enters Politics

It was also during this period that Barbour began courting his first cousin, Lucy Johnson. They had known each other since childhood, and marriage between cousins was not uncommon in that era. They exchanged wedding vows on October 20, 1795, amid a large gathering of family and friends. Within a few years, while dividing his time between his law practice and managing the farmland he had acquired, Barbour announced his intention to seek election to the Virginia House of Delegates. His election in 1798 marked the beginning of a long and distinguished

career in politics.

The fledging United States was struggling with growing pangs of unforeseen political differences springing forth from the new Constitution. A two-party system was forming and the Federalist political party had taken over the presidency and the Congress, bringing with it the repressive "Alien and Sedition Acts." These measures raised constitutional questions about basic freedoms of speech and the press and were strongly opposed by Thomas Jefferson and his fellow Virginian Republicans.

James Barbour quickly became one of the foremost voices of dissent to these laws in the General Assembly, thus drawing considerable attention to himself – an uncommon development for a young freshman legislator. He felt passionately about basic freedoms, keeping government responsible to the people. His political thinking was based on a "strict construction" interpretation of the Constitution; in other words he tried to base his views on the plain words of the text, rather than search for the Framers' possible intent. Over the ensuing years, the high regard bestowed on him by his colleagues in the legislature would continue to place him in the forefront of his partisan peers, first as speaker of the House of Delegates and then as governor of Virginia during the War of 1812.

Barboursville Vineyards is located at the crossroads of State Route 20, between Charlottesville and Orange, and State Route 33, flanked by Gordonsville and Ruckersville.

Family Matters

During these years of rising political stature, Barbour also devoted a comparable amount of energy to the development of his expanding agricultural interests and to his law practice. He and Lucy had four children. Although he was an attentive father, the time he spent with his children was limited by his frequent absences. Yet he was ever mindful of seeing to their personal development. His oldest son, James, was a disappointment. During his initial year at Harvard College, he did well enough academically, but he lacked judgment regarding money matters and discretion in getting along with many of his fellow students. As a consequence, he was suspended.

Other stresses on the family had occurred earlier. The death in late August 1802 of fourteen-month-old Frances cast a pall over the household, but this grief was somewhat allayed two months later by the birth of their second son, Benjamin Johnson. Sadly, he too would not reach adulthood, dying suddenly in mid-summer of 1820, in his eighteenth year. His death was a devastating loss to James and Lucy Barbour, because Benjamin, a scholarly youth and a dutiful son, had shown so much more promise than their elder son, James.

Appointed to the United States Senate

Barbour's two-year term as governor of Virginia during the War of 1812, though traumatic, was served with distinction. In December 1814, he was appointed to the United States Senate by the Virginia legislature. His years of service on the national stage paralleled the careers of many distinguished statesmen such as Daniel Webster, John C. Calhoun, Henry Clay, and the acerbic John Randolph of Roanoke.

While Barbour was serving in the Senate, many issues of extraordinary impact on the country were debated and resolved. Principal among these was the Missouri Compromise, which agitated sectional friction over the issue of slavery.

When John Quincy Adams was elected president in 1824, he appointed Barbour to serve as secretary of war. Much of Barbour's time over the next three years was devoted to studying troubling Indian questions. There was great pressure on the government to revoke existing treaties and to remove to western territories those Indian tribes still living east of the Mississippi River.

Barbour, while mindful of this pressure, sought to bring a degree of fairness and honor in establishing Indian policy. Unfortunately, despite his efforts, this tension ultimately resulted in Indian lands being taken away from them and the limiting of the Adams administration to a single term.

During the final year of his presidency, Adams appointed Barbour minister to the Court of Saint James in London. His diplomatic activities included discussion on boundary and navigational disputes between the United States and Canada and the continuing issue of Britain's impressments of American seamen.

Barbour had a younger brother in politics. Philip Pendleton Barbour was also a lawyer who had the benefit, not afforded to James, of studying under the noted barrister St. George Tucker at the College of William and Mary. Although they held different political convictions, the brothers remained close personally. In 1830, President Andrew Jackson appointed Philip Barbour to a seat on the United States Supreme Court. Interestingly, a cousin, John Strode Barbour from Culpepper County, served in the United States Congress, and like Philip, was a Jacksonian Democrat.

Opposite:
A winter dusting of snow lightly covers the American boxwood and trees surrounding the mansion ruins, where once a serpentine brick wall provided a backdrop to a well-cultivated array of flowers, plants, and shrubbery.

Agrarian Pursuits

With the election of Andrew Jackson, Barbour decided to bring his thirty-year political career to an end. Charles D. Lowery described the Barbours' return home in *James Barbour: A Jeffersonian Republican*: "One late October day in 1829, a travel-weary party returning home from more than a year's sojourn in Europe, topped a crest on the deeply rutted red clay road that led to

Barbour's Virginia farming operations in 1830 consisted of 5,000 acres situated in both Orange and Albemarle counties, along the western base of the Southwest Mountains.

Barboursville." The group consisted of Barbour, his wife, and their youngest daughter, Cornelia.

Spread out before them was a spectacular panoramic view of brilliant scarlets, yellows, and russets dotting the surrounding hills of the Southwest Mountains to their east and the dull blue hues marking the western edge of the Piedmont some thirty miles away at the base of the Blue Ridge Mountains stretching from the South to the North as far as the eye could see. According to Lowery, "Nearby were

Barbour's own terraced fields and fertile bottomlands watered by the meandering Blue Run. Just beyond his view was his large neoclassical country seat, where a happy family reunion awaited him."

Barbour would devote his energy to agrarian pursuits. His success as a planter was not only based on his fondness of the land, but to good management and progressive farming methods. As a result he became one of the wealthiest planters of his region.

Barbour felt a strong obligation to share his innovative scientific agricultural advancements with other planters and small farmers, "to remove the blighting evil of injudicious agriculture." He worked diligently toward eradicating these conditions. In 1836 Barbour proposed to a newly formed Virginia Agricultural Convention two measures that he believed would help bring about improvements.

The first was the creation of a state agricultural board "to promote and coordinate reform and to act as a pressure group to secure from the legislature laws aiding agriculture." The second was to establish an agricultural professorship at the University of Virginia and to create an experimental farm to demonstrate new farming techniques. Although the convention adopted Barbour's recommendations and addressed a petition to the General Assembly, that body took no action.

At the time of his retirement from politics in 1830, he owned 20,000 acres of land, some of which was in scattered parcels as far away as Florida and Mississippi. His 5,000-acre Barboursville operation was situated in both Orange and Albemarle Counties along the western base of the Southwest Mountains.

Over many decades, tobacco had been a principal money crop throughout Virginia, but its cultivation was wearing out the land. Barbour devised methods to control soil erosion and to maintain fertility, thereby allowing him to continue to grow tobacco, but also to add wheat as a major source of cash. In addition to growing various crops, he managed a large herd of merino sheep that provided yet another source of income.

Like many of the wealthy Tidewater planters, particularly during the era before the Revolutionary War, Barbour established a racecourse on his Piedmont plantation. It was located just to the north of his home. At the beginning of the nineteenth century, he acquired Allegrante, a thoroughbred stallion that he bred to increase the quality of his riding and racing stables. His reputation among the devotees of

Opposite: Although these three horses may not have thoroughbred bloodlines tracing back to their forebears in Barbour's once imposing stable, they nevertheless enjoy the same pastures his stallions and mares once grazed.

the turf, such as Henry Clay, ranged throughout the South. Some of his stallions commanded handsome stud fees, one year alone garnering him $5,000.

Maintaining such a diverse and complex farming operation in this plantation, required a sizeable labor force, which in 1830 numbered eighty-one adult slaves.

He, like many in the planter class, condemned the institution of slavery, although did nothing to alleviate the blight this condition had on the Old Dominion and the nation.

Opposite:
Across the spacious fields spread out in front of Montpelier's colonnaded portico are two racecourses that cover about four square miles of this extensive estate. One course is for flat races, the other for steeplechasing and timber jumping.

In 1901, William duPont, Sr., purchased James Madison's former home and farm and set about transforming the property into an expansive hunt country estate. His daughter, Mrs. Marion duPont Scott, founded the Montpelier Hunt Races in 1931 and they continue today.

Above:
Upon Mrs. Scott's death, the property, which had undergone extensive revision during the duPont ownership, passed into the stewardship of the National Trust for Historic Preservation.
Today, after several years of architectural restoration, the Montpelier mansion has reverted to the configuration and design James and Dolley Madison would recognize.

The Mansion

The crowning jewel of Barbour's estate was the imposing neo-classical mansion, with its commanding view of the Blue Ridge Mountains, designed by his multi-talented neighbor, friend, and mentor, Thomas Jefferson. In a letter dated March 1817, James Barbour wrote to Jefferson: "The bearers of this, James Bradley and Edward Ancel, are undertakers of my building – the former, a

This early rendering, discovered in the rare book section of the Alderman Library at the University of Virginia, illustrates the southwest frontage of the Barboursville complex prior to the devastating fire Christmas Day, 1884. Note the large open space beyond the buildings where Barbour had his racetrack.

carpenter; the latter, bricklayer. I have resolved on the plan you were good enough to present me and for which I return you my sincere thanks. You were kind enough to accompany the plan with a suggestion that it would be well for my workmen to see your building and receive such verbal explanations as might facilitate their labors. To that end I have directed them to repair to Monticello."

Jefferson had purchased his first book on architecture from a bookseller by the front gate in the college yard while a student at the College of William and Mary.

Roman architecture had a strong influence on him, particularly his reaction at seeing the Maison Carrée in Nimes, France, while serving as minister to that country. It became the inspiration for his design of the Virginia Capitol in Richmond.

Jefferson had long been an avid disciple of the noted sixteenth-century Italian architect, Andrea Palladio. He incorporated many elements from the Villa Rotunda and other classic Palladian masterpieces into his extraordinary estate at Monticello and into his design for the University of Virginia.

Jefferson designed a number of homes for friends, but with Barboursville, he incorporated many features that are reminiscent of Monticello. There was a two-story octagonal drawing room, which projected south under a large pediment portico overlooking a three-acre formal garden that formed into a geometric pattern. There was a serpentine brick wall providing a backdrop to the well-cultivated array of flowers, plants, and shrubbery, a feature that can be found in

Opposite: A late afternoon warm sun helps to highlight the southern portico and one of the exterior sides distinguishing Monticello's parlor and dome room.

Below, left: Thomas Jefferson was a serious disciple of Palladio and incorporated many of the architect's distinguishing features in his design for the University of Virginia, Monticello, Barboursville, and other buildings. The Villa Capra or La Rotunda, built as pleasure pavilion just outside of Vicenza, was a favorite of Jefferson's. Its elegant design has been used all over the world.

Below, right: Famed sixteenth century Italian architect, Andrea Palladio, designed an enclosed market arcade to protect his fellow Vicenza citizens from the elements. An arch within the arcade frames his statue.

This portrait of Thomas Jefferson by Charles Willson Peale, 1791-1792, is one of many rendered from life over the years by the artist.

the gardens at the University of Virginia. The matching north portico opened into a hallway of equal height to the drawing room. Although Jefferson had included a dome into the design, it was never built.

Barboursville, like Monticello, was built where a slight downward slope in the land allowed for the two-story structure to have the appearance of a single story house. This was most apparent when approaching from the principal north

Opposite:
A new day, the sun will soon dissipate the September fog. Thousands of starlings fly over the Barbour mansion.

entryway. From the central portion of the house extended east and west wings in which four large bedrooms were situated.

Not far from the main house were located several dependencies. There was a kitchen, an icehouse, a carriage house, a long row of stables, and the slave quarters.

An old farm road traverses down from the cupola topped winery on past the circa 1900 red sheep barn, before winding around the ruins of the mansion and The 1804 Inn.

There were two buildings, now connected, a short distance to the west of the manor, which served as the residence for the Barbours before the construction of Barboursville. They may have also been designed by Jefferson and are identified with the year 1804, the time the first tax payment was recorded. Currently they serve as a small luxury inn.

It is not certain when Philip Mazzei sat for this portrait by Jacques - Louis David. It may have been around 1790 while he was in Paris. David was the court painter to Louis XVI and Napoleon Bonaparte.

Philip Mazzei: A Man for All Seasons

Thomas Jefferson's long and well-documented interest in architecture was matched by his love for good wine. This interest was certainly intensified in 1773 with the arrival at the Virginia Capes of Philip Mazzei and a small band of fellow Italian vignerons (winemakers). Mazzei was a forty-three year old multi-faceted Florentine nobleman with a broad sweep of interests and accomplishments. He was a surgeon, merchant, linguist, diplomatic agent, historian, and a royal advisor who would become a naturalized citizen of Virginia and Poland. Yet it was as a horticulturist that he was making his way to the Old Dominion.

While working in 1767 as a merchant in London, Mazzei met Benjamin Franklin, who introduced him to Thomas Adams, a businessman from Virginia. Through this connection, Mazzei met other Virginians who were living in London and began establishing commercial relationships with wealthy planters from the Old Dominion. By 1771, Mazzei proposed a plan for Adams, Jefferson, and a number of others, to import 10,000 grapevines from several locales in France, Italy, Spain, and Portugal for shipment to the colonies. In this plan 1,000 vines would be consigned to Augusta County in the Valley of Virginia "where hills and risen ground favor the cultivation of the vine and olive trees."

On December 2, 1773, the *Virginia Gazette* announced the arrival in the James River of the frigate *Triumph* from Livorno, with Philip Mazzei and a number of gentlemen on board ". . . in order to settle and cultivate vines in this colony." The General Assembly was in session in Williamsburg at the time, and, upon his arrival there, Mazzei was greeted by, among many others, George Washington and George Wythe, the distinguished lawyer and teacher who later signed the Declaration of Independence.

The galls visible on the lower side of this wild grape leaf are a sign of a recent attack by Phylloxera. The vine will survive as its ancestors have for millennia. (photo taken on July 13, 2006 in the woods of Barboursville).

A Virginia State historic marker provides mute, cryptic confirmation of Mazzei's early efforts at viticulture in the Old Dominion.

En route to the Valley, Mazzei and Adams stopped at Monticello, where, before breakfast, Jefferson used his persuasive talents to convince his guests this was the place to cultivate their vines. Mazzei recalled in his memoirs that Jefferson "learned that the adjoining 400 acres belonged to a 'poor farmer' who could not afford slaves." He then offered Mazzei a gift of 2,000 acres to add to the tract he would purchase. There was a cottage suitable for Mazzei's workers and he promptly built a house for himself and named it "Colle," which in Italian translates into "saddle" or "ridge of a hill."

Another notable event took place in Mazzei's life shortly thereafter. He had become quite friendly with a French widow, a Madame Marie Martin, while in London. She and her daughter accompanied him to Virginia. Thomas Adams persuaded Mazzei to marry the French widow, "lest he be thought to be cohabiting with her, thereby jeopardizing his reputation and the daughter's prospects of a good marriage." Marriage vows were exchanged, but it was not to be a happy relationship.

"I Have Not Said Much About My Agriculture"

The degree of success Mazzei had with his experimental vineyard and wine making is not fully known because he became caught up by the political events of the day. In 1774, Mazzei was naturalized as a Virginia citizen by the Colony's Royal Governor, Lord Dunmore. He was frequently absent from Colle in order to follow developments in Williamsburg. He wrote of these matters with a degree of regret. "I have not said much about my agriculture, for I did not attend to it as I should have, because the great public issue occupied almost all of my time."

Indeed, Mazzei played an important role before and during the American Revolution. With the threat of British military action in Hampton, Virginia, Mazzei signed up as a private in the "Independent Company" of Albemarle. Before this unit could deploy to Hampton, the British had withdrawn. Patrick Henry urged them to disband and insisted that Mazzei could best help the cause with his pen and oratory.

Mazzei also shared his political views with his close friend Jefferson and recalled that Jefferson "would send me those of his reflections on which he wished to hear my opinion."

In the years between 1774 and 1776, Mazzei's interest in Virginia's political affairs gained momentum. He spoke out against British rule and wrote articles in Italian under the pseudonym Furioso, which Jefferson translated into English for publication in the *Virginia Gazette*. One of these articles read in part:

"My dear fellow citizens, to reach the goal we desire we must remember that the natural rights of man are the basis of a free government. This discourse will clearly show that Briton was never this type of state, even at her highest level of perfection, and that ours may become no more than a captive copy of it, with all its other disadvantages, causing it to become little more than a state of slavery. . . All men are by nature equally free and independent. Such equality is necessary in order to create a free government. All men must be equal to each other in natural law. This equality is necessary to establish a

free government. Each one must be equal to the other in natural rights. Class distinctions are not always static and will always be nothing more than an effective stumbling block, and the reason is most clear. Whenever you have many classes of men in one nation, it is necessary that you give each one its share in the government; otherwise one class will tyrannize the others. But the shares cannot be made perfectly equal; and whenever one class takes power, human events will demonstrate that the classes are not in balance; and bit by bit the greater part of the machine will collapse."

This statement has been judged by some to be the inspiration for Thomas Jefferson's immortal words, "All men are created equal," found in the Declaration of Independence. This may have resulted in Mazzei's receiving one of five reportedly copied drafts of the Declaration of Independence made by Jefferson for his friends. Mazzei later presented his copy to Countess Noaille de Tess, an aunt of the Marquis de Lafayette. Unfortunately, this copy has been lost to posterity.

Mazzei's contributions, both in his writings and other contributions to the early birth pangs of the nation, may not be well known today. One reason might be traced to a letter he wrote June 16, 1776, to Virginia Lieutenant-Governor John Page: "My composition is in Italian with English words. You know that what is elegance in one language is sometimes nonsense in another. . . it is entirely owing to a very little remnant of modesty that I don't desire you to publish that I am the Author of them. I am clear in my principles and I am ready to support them."

Among many contributions Mazzei made to the patriot's cause was to return to Italy in an effort to raise money for Virginia. Governor Patrick Henry, Thomas Jefferson, George Mason, and others asked him in late 1778 to appeal to his friend, the Grand Duke of Tuscany, for some much needed funds. Although he was unsuccessful in this undertaking, he remained in Europe for four years serving as an agent for Virginia.

The General's Horses Trample the Vineyard

While Mazzei was on this mission, his home Colle was rented to Hessian General Baron Friedreich von Riedesel, who had surrendered in 1777 along with British General John Burgoyne after the battle of Saratoga. Charlottesville had been selected as a remote location to house the prisoners taken in this American victory and they remained there from January 1779 until October 1780. Shortly after taking up residence, the general's horses trampled over the vineyard Mazzei had set out, destroying a labor of five or six years and putting an end to the experiment in wine growing.

The portrait of Thomas Jefferson in the winery's barrel aging room, named for its elite wine Octagon, is a reminder of his love of and passion for the fascinating world of wine.

Upon his return in 1784, Mazzei visited George Washington, George Mason, and a number of prominent patriots before returning to Europe for new adventures. Interestingly, he left his wife, whom he described as being "obstinate and indecent." Madame Mazzei died in 1788, and, although there is no marker to be seen today, she is buried in the Jefferson family graveyard at Monticello. In the subsequent years Mazzei continued to stay in contact with his many friends in America, frequently serving as a source for horticultural advice.

"An Anglican Monarchical Aristocratical Party"

Jefferson, in turn, kept Philip Mazzei apprised of current events. In a letter dated April 24, 1796, Jefferson wrote from Monticello: ". . . The aspect of our politics has wonderfully changed since you left us. In place of that noble love of liberty and republican government which carried us triumphantly through the war, an Anglican monarchical aristocratical party has sprung up, whose avowed object is to draw over us the substance, as they have already done the forms, of the British government."

Jefferson shared these private thoughts with fellow Republicans, but Mazzei, without Jefferson's knowledge or permission, passed these words on to several acquaintances. As a result, they found their way into print, much to the political detriment of Jefferson at the time. Yet this position helped form a new political faction. These views would be echoed by James Barbour to members of the Virginia legislature two years later.

It is interesting to reflect on how this position marked the beginning of the two-party system in the United States, while also linking the political views of Jefferson, Barbour, and Mazzei. It is not unlike how these three were united in a shared vision of bringing forth a more productive use of the land through innovative farming activity and in finding ways of retaining soil fertility in order to develop improved varieties of plants, trees, and vines.

In 1805, Mazzei provided Benjamin Latrobe, the architect of the new United States Capitol, with two sculptors to carve figures for the building. Latrobe that same year, mindful of Mazzei's early attempts at viticulture, was led to prophesy, "The time is already approaching when our vines. . . will spread your name and gratitude over a great portion of our country."

An early spring prospect of Monticello's southern front provides a clear view of the great lawn, bordered by the serpentine walk and the first of the roundabout roads. During Jefferson's day his "little mountain" was always a work in progress.

"And Abundance of Lean and Meager Spots of Stony Red Soil"

That Jefferson appreciated Mazzei's viticultural experiment was evident when he wrote in 1811, ". . . .the Italian Mazzei, who came here to make wine, fixed on these South West mountains, having a South East aspect, and abundance of lean and meager spots of stony red soil, without sand, I am inclined to believe he was right in preferring the South Eastern face of this ridge of mountains."

Jefferson's own efforts paralleled Mazzei's attempts at establishing wine-producing grapes. In 1766, when he was twenty-one, Jefferson began keeping a garden book. While he was in Williamsburg attending the 1770 session of the House of Burgesses, he made his first notation regarding viticulture, and he

The tiny white clabbered Church of the Brethren looks out over rolling rows of grapes at the southern side of the vineyard. Every half hour melodic sounds of bells from the church's carillon float out over the countryside.

acknowledged receiving some grapevines from his old law mentor, George Wythe. A brief entry on March 28 of the next year noted, "planted 5 grapes from N. Lewis's on S.E. edge of garden." Again, on April 2, 1773, "planted 30 vines just below where the new garden wall will run." These were set out by some Tuscan vignerons who had accompanied Mazzei.

Frustration, even to this day, comes to the husbandman. On May 5, 1774, Jefferson recorded a killing frost that destroyed almost everything, ". . . it killed the wheat, rye, corn, many tobacco plants, and even large saplings. The leaves of the trees were entirely killed, all shoots of vines." He went on to report the frost affected all of Virginia and the neighboring colonies.

The Susceptibility of European Grapes

Four years later, Jefferson hired several men to work in his orchard and vineyards. Anthony Giannini, a vigneron who had accompanied Mazzei from Italy, was to play a leading role. Jefferson's Garden Book of 1788 includes a detailed drawing showing 561 vines planted three feet apart in an area 100 by 100 feet. For all these efforts, over many years there would be continued failure with vine growing at Monticello. Neglect was a major factor, thanks to Jefferson's frequent absences while serving the new nation, but in addition to neglect and the occasional frost, the European varietals were susceptible to fatal assaults from insects and disease.

In late spring 1784, Jefferson left Virginia for Paris to serve as one of the three commissioners sent to negotiate treaties with the French government. He was gone for four years. Fortunately, he was able to travel extensively during this period. In the spring of 1787, he toured a number of wine producing provinces in the south of France studying wine production and reporting on farming operations.

Included in this extensive three-month journey was a brief swing through the countryside of northern Italy. Just west of Milan, Jefferson made note in his travel journal of the unusual method of planting vines: "Along rows of trees they lash poles from tree to tree. Between the trees are set vines which passing over the pole, are carried on the pole of the next row, whose vines are in a like manner brought to this, and twined together; thus forming intervals between the rows of trees alternately into arbors, and open space." He had gathered a great store of knowledge that he hoped to put to good use. After returning to Paris, he reflected on his experience in a letter to his nephew Peter Carr in Virginia, saying that "travel made men wiser, but less happy."

Thomas Jefferson's many contributions to society and the public good are well known. Less well understood are those of James Barbour and Philip Mazzei. Nevertheless both men added lasting values to Virginia and to the nation's development, particularly in the field of horticulture. Mazzei died March 19, 1816, in his native Tuscany at the age of eighty-five. He is buried in Pisa. His home, Colle, was demolished in 1933. A state highway marker situated near the site a few miles east of Charlottesville provides mute evidence of his attempt to cultivate vinifera varietals in the region.

Opposite: Peter's Mountain, overlooking the Barboursville Vineyards, was named after Thomas Jefferson's father whose landholdings once extended some twenty miles east along the Southwest Mountains from his home in Albemarle County.

Gianni and Silvana Zonin Visit Monticello in 1976

Some two hundred years after both Mazzei and Jefferson determined that excellent wine could be produced in the foothills of the Blue Ridge Mountains their dream is being fully realized. Gianni and Silvana Zonin learned of the vision of these two brilliant men while visiting Monticello from their native Italy during the Bicentennial year of 1976. The couple was so impressed with the efforts of these pioneering viticulturists that they determined to unearth, both literally and figuratively, why vinifera grapes had failed to grow two centuries earlier.

Gianni Zonin is president of the Zonin Family Wines and Estates, headquartered in Gambellara, in Northern Italy. He and his family own eleven prestigious properties in seven Italian regions, ranging from Venezia to Sicily, and produce dozens of prize-winning wines made from international and Italian native varietals. They have an impressive 4,400 acres under vine, making the Zonin Family Wines and Estates Italy's most important family-run wine company.

In addition to their commitment to producing great varietals, which led the Zonins to expand their operations internationally, Gianni and Silvana Zonin have a love of and commitment to historic preservation. This love of old houses and

"Here, I take a quiet moment with my wife, Silvana, at the well on the south lawn of our home at this estate, having just opened it as The 1804 Inn.
Everywhere one might turn, her inexhaustibly welcoming hand had translated the generous and celebratory vision of wine growing into innumerable expressions of amenity and beauty, and had restored the estate to its historic peerage in hospitality with Monticello and Montpelier.
The passion for fine wine is truly not divisible from a love for the beauty of the land and its traditions. It was no wonder, as the promise of Octagon was being realized in the vineyards, that this labor of love had also polished the estate, in all its aspects, in a glowing welcome."

Gianni Zonin

Gianni Zonin with his sons: Francesco, Michele, and Domenico

estates has led the couple to take on many restoration projects, and eventually led them to Barboursville. When they were first married in Vicenza they lived with his uncle in his home, Montebello, which was built in 1707. Vicenza is a city abounding with matchless architecture, largely created by Andrea Palladio.

The Zonin Family farms over 4,000 acres, in eleven estates, over seven regions.

Castello d'Albola, situated in the Chianti section of Tuscany, is the crown jewel of the eleven renown Zonin wine-producing estates scattered throughout the seven viticultural regions of Italy.

Castello d'Albola: Home To Many of Tuscany's Most Important Families

In 1979 the Zonins acquired the Castello d'Albola estate located in Radda, an ancient little town in the Chianti region of Tuscany. Over the centuries it has been owned by many of Tuscany's important families. The history of this Tuscan zone is a very long one. The exact origin of the name "Chianti" is hard to pinpoint. It may have derived from the Etruscan family of Clantes, who lived in the area between the seventh and eighth centuries B.C., and who introduced the cultivation of vines into the region.

Although this majestic castle, perched on the crest of a hill, with a commanding panoramic vista of surrounding vineyards, is a prime example of Renaissance architecture, the grounds are guarded by an even older medieval structure, a twelfth-century tower. This extraordinary complex is the brightest star among the eleven vineyard estates in the Zonin constellation.

"At Castello d'Albola I am a Custodian of the Territory"

"I have always felt that there is a difference between being owner of a property and custodian of a property," said Gianni Zonin in reflecting on acquiring the Castello d'Albola estate. "At Castello d'Albola I am a custodian of the territory. I too have been infected by the Chianti 'bug.' The area has cast its unmistakable spell over me and I haven't been able to shake it off. More than twenty years have passed since those late winter days when I wandered from village to village, from farm to farm, looking for an estate into which I could transplant my dreams or, more concretely, my ambitions.

"I turned up at Pian d'Albola almost by chance, by mistake. Time seemed to have stood still, leaving pretty well everything unchanged: the sixteenth-century house that had once belonged to the Acciaiolis, to the De'Pazzis, to the Samminiatis, and to the Ginori Contis; the fertile vineyards magnificently exposed to the south; the ruins of the farmhouses that had once been the lively scene of passions and precise labors. It was love at first sight. I immediately understood that this corner of Chianti could be given new life, a modern form of productivity, and that its inhabitants could be given a new gratifying employment opportunity. After a mere three days I had completed the purchase. And so the adventure began. . . ."

"This is our home away from home," says Silvana Zonin."We have spent time every summer here for more than two decades and always fill the castle's tower guest rooms with visiting friends and family." Their sons, Domenico, Francesco, and Michele spent much of their childhood there exploring the countryside.

Slender cypress cedars flank a gently sloping prospect of newly budding grape leaves from the Castello d'Albola estate.

An ornate lantern, one of a pair suspended out from Castello d'Albola to illuminate the front entry, frames the estate's small chapel cross.

". . . Starting a Vineyard In The United States"

In the early 1970s, Gianni Zonin had been thinking seriously of starting a vineyard in the United States. As a young man in 1961, he had visited a number of the major viticultural estates: Taylor Winery in New York; Roma,

Gallo, Louis Martini, and Christian Brothers in California; and Mogan David in Chicago.

While touring California, Zonin met Dr. Harold Olmo, a professor of viticulture at the University of California at Davis. Zonin recalled, "He was considered the most important professor in viticulture in the world and had a discerning eye for land that should produce wine-growing grapes."

". . . And I Fell in Love with Virginia!"

"We then began our tour of the Old Dominion. It was spring, the dogwood was in flower; it was wonderful," recalled Zonin, "and I fell in love with Virginia! I asked several people about temperature in winter, spring, summer, and autumn and then contacted Dr. Olmo to ask his opinion on the possibilities of planting vinifera grapes in Virginia. He said, 'It is possible, but it is better in the Napa Valley of California.' He also suggested the small town of Roseburg, Oregon, as probably the best place to plant grapes."

Although Zonin was well aware of the successful wine operations in the Napa and Sonoma Valleys, he determined after several weeks that the Piedmont area of Virginia possessed a perfect soil and microclimate that was not unlike many of the outstanding wine-growing regions of Italy. He also realized that it would be much easier to fly from Italy to Virginia than from Italy to California.

Zonin visited several dozen Virginia estates before seeing Barboursville, and shortly thereafter he purchased the 850-acre property. For some years it had been a sheep farm. When it was mentioned to the farm manager that their plan was to start a vineyard, the manger said, "Virginia is good only for sheep," then on reflection added, "If not sheep, then tobacco."

Upon seeing the Barboursville ruins, the Zonins, with the encouragement from noted University of Virginia professor of architecture, Fred Nichols, at first thought to restore the manor to the original Jefferson creation. Realizing that as practical matter this would be a difficult undertaking, they focused on restoring the adjacent buildings that pre-dated the one destroyed by fire, with the idea of transforming them into a charming, diminutive inn.

Opposite:
One can but marvel on how beautiful these rooms must have been furnished prior to the 1884 Christmas Day fire.
The Barbours would have frequently extended their gracious hospitality to visiting friends, politicians, and travelers alike. This warm-hearted generosity, in keeping with the traditions of the day, would have sparked spirited conversations ranging from thoroughbred racing, crop rotation, the Indian question, and concerns about the slavery issue.

April, 1978
Gianni Zonin (left), always upbeat, here expresses the pleasure that comes from planting.

"We Produced Three Bottles of Cabernet Sauvignon"

The next task was to find a manager. Gabriele Rausse, an agronomist, had recently arrived from Australia and was working on an estate in the area. "An agreement was worked out," said Zonin, "and we immediately plowed some soil on April 13, 1976. Two years later we produced three bottles of Cabernet Sauvignon! We still conserve these three bottles."

"Gabriele Rausse is a wonderful man, a wonderful agronomist, although he did not have, at that time, a deep wine- making experience " Zonin recalled, "so when we started to produce grapes, we felt it was necessary to hire a winemaker." At about this same time, a gentleman who lived near Monticello, on the old property of Philip Mazzei, asked Gabriele to work for him. Today Gabriele Rausse owns a successful boutique winery very close to Thomas Jefferson's Monticello.

Upper left: In April, 1976, Zonin (left) with Gabriele Rausse (center) and his friend, Count Cigogna (right), studying the texture and composition of what is, for them, a fascinating and unexplored soil.

Upper right: Zonin is pictured with his brother Giuseppe (left) and the Barbour mansion ruins in the background, completely overgrown with vines and trees. The ruins have been tended and preserved properly ever since, and have become a magnet to travelers on Virginia's Constitution Highway.

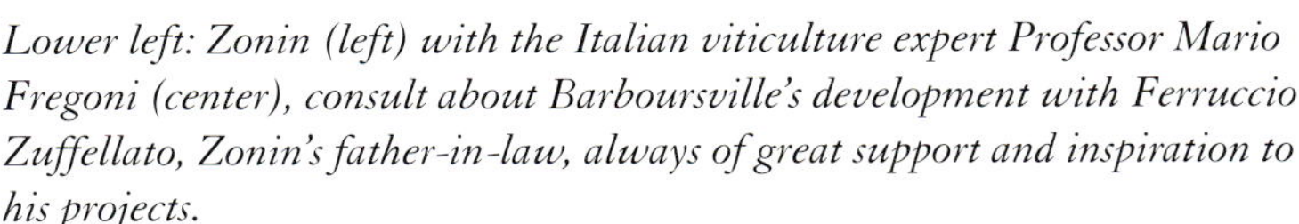

Lower left: Zonin (left) with the Italian viticulture expert Professor Mario Fregoni (center), consult about Barboursville's development with Ferruccio Zuffellato, Zonin's father-in-law, always of great support and inspiration to his projects.

Lower right: April, 1976. Zonin was fascinated with a native, wild vine growing a short distance from where he would soon be planting Euoropean vines.

A new winemaker was brought over from Italy, but this move was not satisfactory either, and Zonin had to change many farm managers before finding the right person for Barboursville. He met Luca Paschina in 1990 and asked him if he would be interested in traveling to Barboursville Vineyards to make recommendations about what needed to be done to make it into a successful operation. Luca spent that September and October working with the harvest and then returned to Italy. Zonin, more than pleased with Luca's report and talent, offered him the position of general manager and winemaker. Luca, for his part, captivated by his experience and the possibilities Barboursville presented, accepted the job and returned a short time later.

Below: Inaugurated on August 25, 2007, the Octagon Cellar contains more than 100 barrels of wine in ideal aging conditions and a permanent exhibit on the history of wine-making in Virginia.

Opposite: Created for the first time in 1991 and released in 1996 to celebrate the twentieth anniversary of the winery, Octagon is the wine which has come to distinguish and define Virginia as a great wine region.

OCTAGON
2004
VIRGINIA
JAMES BARBOUR ESTATE PLAN
BARBOURSVILLE
Vineyards

"If I Have a Choice, I prefer to be First in Virginia"

In characterizing his philosophy, Zonin points out, "It is better to be first in Virginia than second in California. Barboursville is developing and increasing in the vineyards, in the winery, and in the beauty. It is an exciting

Luca Paschina (left) pictured with former Virginia Governor Mark Warner at the Governor's Mansion. Governor Warner, a Virginia grape grower himself, presented the honors to Luca Paschina for the 2001 Octagon, the gold medal recipient.

Luca Paschina converses with the President of Italy, Giorgio Napolitano, (left) during his visit to Washington in December, 2007. The vineyards' premier wines, Octagon and Malvaxia, were served at the gala that evening.

experience. If I have a choice, I prefer to be first in Virginia."

He cites three major accomplishments that have occurred at Barboursville: "First, when I got the first Gold Medal for best wine in Virginia with Cabernet Sauvignon Reserve. Second, when Barboursville received the very important Governor's Cup award several years ago. Third, when the Commonwealth of Virginia named Luca Paschina "Virginia Wine Industry Person of the Year."

Honors continue to accumulate. On May 4, 2007, Her Majesty Queen Elizabeth II of Great Britain paid a return visit to Virginia to honor the 400th anniversary of the establishment of the Jamestown colony. Upon her arrival at the newly restored Virginia State Capitol she attended a welcoming reception in the Governor's Mansion. Chosen to best represent the culinary and wine arts were the Inn at Little Washington and Barboursville Vineyards with its Octagon 2001 vintage.

After the reception at the Governor's Mansion, where Barboursville wines were served, Queen Elizabeth traveled once again to Jamestown, where some five decades earlier her presence acknowledged the early English efforts at colonization. While in Williamsburg, she was entertained by the Colonial Williamsburg Foundation and extended her best wishes to her Virginia hosts before touring the Sir Christopher Wren building at the College of William and Mary.

Viticultural Philosophy

In the wake of the California wines' shocking success at the now-famous Paris Wine Tasting of 1976, the international spotlight was cast upon modern American winemaking for the first time. Though seemingly brand-new to outsiders, the seeds of West Coast viticulture were sown generations before. The same, too, can be said of Barboursville Vineyards. The first European vines (*Vitis vinifera*) since the days of Thomas Jefferson were successfully planted at Barboursville in 1976, yet the pedigree of both the vines and wine making reach back through eight generations of Zonin family success in Italy. Hence, although there was no ready guide to grape growing in Virginia — aside from the notes of Jefferson's contemporary, the Italian émigré Philip Mazzei, who documented his own futile efforts — Barboursville's early years can be described as learned, rather than blind, experimentation.

For much of the first two decades, the estate was meticulously planted and replanted as the nuances of Barboursville's terrain and microclimate were discovered. It takes two to three years for new vines to come into full production, and then the patience of at least another five vintages to measure the success of those

The harvest has just started and the first bins of pinot grigio, the earliest ripening variety, are on their way to the cellar to be pressed.

Left: Early morning, the air is crisp and the Nebbiolo grapes in the Goodlow mountain vineyard have reached a desired stage of ripening.

Right:The hand holding the cluster above the earth stands as a reminder that wine is a craft resulting from harmony between land and man.

plantings against the unpredictable Virginia weather. In short, an entire decade can be spent determining if you've planted the right grape on the ideal vineyard site, or an unsuitable variety altogether.

Each passing year widened the knowledge base while narrowing the scope of compatible clones, root stocks, and trellising systems. Cool climate grapes and warm climate grapes were given equal opportunity in the beginning, though it didn't take long to see that the latter are better suited to the region. By the 1990s, Virginia was revealing her true likes and dislikes, and the viticultural team was busy selecting the best exposure sites and matching soil types to varietal. Furthermore, as Barboursville approached its thirtieth anniversary, winemaker Luca Paschina declared a moratorium on untested grape varieties: "There are over 500 varieties in Italy alone . . . plenty to experiment with within our heritage. There is curiosity, but it would be an endless research. Why not focus on what works? We're pulling up Pinot Noir and putting in the perfectly suited Cabernet Franc."

The Future is Now

Just as Mazzei and Jefferson were trailblazers, so, too, are Gianni Zonin and Luca Paschina. When familiar techniques did not exactly apply, they were adapted. Thus, a new way was created. . . the Virginia way. With the improvisation of the 1970s and 1980s behind, the future of Virginian viticulture is no longer a gamble. Thanks to breakthrough vineyard management and

August 8, 2006
This picture was taken at the beginning of the 2006 harvest and what appeared to be an ideal ripening season could only but elicit smiles.
From left, to right, Francesco Baravalle, Fernando Franco, Gianni Zonin, and Luca Paschina.

intrepid fertilizing, small plantings prove new concepts that can be duplicated widely and efficiently.

For instance, viticultural thinking has shifted from tons per acre to pounds per vine. Once, a vineyard's production was measured according to grapes per acre. However, this method does not address a more fundamental concern: crop load. Five hundred plants producing three tons of grapes are doing a lot more work than 1,500 hundred plants producing the same three tons. To craft high-quality wines, yields per vine must be optimized. By planting vines closely together and training them to ripen fewer grape clusters, the aromas and flavors are concentrated. The future is now in perfecting the varieties themselves. With five clones of Cabernet Franc currently planted, their individual performance can be tracked over the years. When it comes time to plant more, only the choicest clone will be propagated. Already, clone 181 has been identified as the top Merlot . . . for Cabernet Sauvignon, it is clone 337.

Traditional vs. Trendy: Steel Nerves, Steel Tanks

In order to survive, winemakers in the United States have to balance what they like to make with what the American palate likes to drink. Trendsetters are the wine-industry chameleons; modifying grapes and wine-making styles like hem lengths. Traditionalists, on the other hand, care less about the season's hot trends, sticking to classics that never go out of fashion. Behemoth wineries producing millions of bottles are beholden to what's selling at the moment, whereas boutique wineries proudly supply a niche market making slow food wines, not fast food wines.

As with fads on the runway, fashions in wine also come back around sooner or later. In the case of Chardonnay, for example, many New World vintners jumped on the oak and malolactic bandwagon in the 1980s, subjecting their wines to palate-fatiguing levels of toasted wood and sweet cream. Today, there is a movement back to the European ideal of crisp, mineral-driven Chardonnays known more for elegance than power. Winemakers currently turning to stainless steel fermentation and away from excessive barrel aging are championing the very style of Chardonnay that Barboursville has stalwartly produced since 1978. Paschina has always believed that "Chardonnay shines without oak barrels. We didn't invent this style, it's how Italy's been drinking for decades. Instead of giving in to fashion, we stuck to tradition . . . we still do."

As for red wines, professional and casual oenophiles alike are familiar with the lambasting that Merlot underwent in the 2004 vinous hit movie, *Sideways*. Pinot Noir sales spiked after the film's release, but Merlot never slowed, and it still ranks as the largest red varietal, ahead of Cabernet Sauvignon in U.S. sales. In Bordeaux, legendary Merlot-based blends have been made for centuries. Like the vaunted Chateaux Petrus, Haut-Brion, and Cheval Blanc, Barboursville's top *cuvée*, Octagon, will continue to be produced principally from Merlot, regardless of trends or movies. According to Paschina, "In wine, thousands of years of tradition trickle down. With research and technology transferring between wineries, techniques become more globalized; there is less distinction. Still, the most valuable information goes mouth-to-mouth."

Now, while many New World winemakers often strive for extreme Brix and alcohol levels, vignerons in the Old World tradition know that blockbuster wines may win modern competitions, but they are notoriously unfriendly to food. With all that wine wisdom between them, Gianni Zonin and Luca Paschina were on a quest to produce wines that exhibited Italian verve and Virginian character. They've succeeded.

The Winemaker

Luca Paschina moved from one Piedmont to another. Born in Torino, it is fitting that his birth year, 1961, is also one of the classic post-war European vintages. A second-generation winemaker, Paschina earned a

degree in oenology from Alba's Institute Umberto I in 1982, and then sharpened his technique and philosophy on and off Italian soil over the next eight years. In 1990, he was approached by Gianni Zonin to consult at Barboursville Vineyards. With his recently retired father covering for him in Italy, Paschina spent September and October involved in his first Virginia harvest. Upon returning to Italy, Paschina was offered the helm. Impassioned by Barboursville's history, pastoral beauty, and wine-growing promise, Paschina was back in Virginia three days later. "To create a great wine region, you must produce wines of distinction and ageability for several vintages. With our Octagon, we have discovered an important wine and made Virginia a true wine region," observes Zonin.

2002
NEBBIOLO
OCTAG
2002
VIRGINIA

VIRGINIA HISTORIC LANDMARK
2002
VIRGINIA
CABERNET FRANC
RESERVE

The Viticulturist

Fernando Franco, like the vines themselves, is firmly rooted to Barboursville's beauty and excitement. His understanding of the Virginia soil and climate began in 1983, making him one of the Commonwealth's most experienced viticulturists. Born in the village of Armenia, Franco cultivated his interest in agronomy in rich soils along the chain of El Salvador's ancient volcanoes. He joined Barboursville

Fernando Franco (right) and Luca Paschina observe closely and with curiosity the clusters on a Cabernet Franc vine, recently planted, in its first year of bearing fruit.

Vineyards in 1997 after a soccer friend made the introduction. A jovial man who smiles even when the rains come, Franco's motto embodies a lifestyle as much as his philosophy of vineyard management: "Treat

To Kim it was good for me to have you
Here I will miss you
See you soon again

The smile of Donald Foster (left) is hiding behind his mustache. Countless are the loads of grapes that he has delivered through the years from the vineyards to the cellar.

Benito Barron (right) is among several of our vignerons from Central America that for years have made it possible for Barboursville Vineyards to cultivate vines successfully.

Grapes are being hauled to the cellar, a good reason to celebrate! Rogelio Martinez on the left, Donald Foster behind, and Santiago Vega on the right.

Benito Barron carefully selects each cluster of Nebbiolo. Any blemished or a not perfectly ripe cluster will be left behind.

vines like people . . . with love and respect."

The wisest winemakers, Paschina included, acknowledge that great wines are made in the vineyards, and Franco is Barboursville's liaison between the hills and the cellar. When the climate is kind, his job is to shepherd vines from bud break to harvest without squandering qualities that the sunshine and soil have imbued. However, it's in the face of heat waves, cold fronts, and cloudbursts that Franco earns his stripes as vine doctor and authority of plant physiology and pathology. When others are gnashing teeth over dreary weather reports, Franco is busy bolstering his vines' own natural defenses. In that sense, he's the grapewhisperer: "I can determine by looking at the leaves what the vines need." Like Paschina, Franco is a traditionalist at heart, leaning on technology when appropriate, but never bringing a heavy hand of chemicals or fertilizers that disturb the delicate interplay of soil and plant: "Develop balanced vineyards and you get balanced wines." Ten vintages into his Barboursville tenure, Franco's idealism is refreshingly apparent: "That's the beauty of it, each year is different. And we haven't yet made the best wine I believe we can make."

Harvest 2007
Associate winemaker Francesco Baravalle is ecstatic about the color and the effusively fragrant aromas.

The Restaurant

Thomas Jefferson's designs are inseparable from his beloved Virginia, but sources of his inspiration reach back to northeast Italy, where the Zonin family has called home for eight generations. There, in the province of Veneto, the architectural masterworks of Andrea Palladio have been revered since the Renaissance. Jefferson discovered Palladio's Four Books on Architecture and began infusing Roman

Wheels of sheep cheese age in Pat Elliott's cave. Since its inception, the Palladio Restaurant has been proudly using this local Orange County product not simply because of its provenance but especially because of its superior quality.

classicalism into his own buildings. Today, Palladian details found at Monticello and the University of Virginia are echoed in the Barbour mansion and the winery's vineyard-side arcades.

Given how Palladio's torch was carried to Barboursville by both Jefferson and the Zonin family, it is appropriate that his name is honored every time the menu is perused at Palladio Restaurant. And whether in the intimate Veranda Room (an al fresco porch enclosed by French doors) or the Dining Room (with views overlooking the ruins and vineyards), fine dining is punctuated by shadows of a 100-year-old willow oak and rare prints of Palladio's sixteenth-century Teatro Olimpico.

Below: Michael Clark of Planet Earth Diversified from neighboring Green County is capable, with his hydroponic greenhouses, of supplying the restaurant all year round with the most tender, flavorful, and freshly cut microgreens.

Opposite: One may almost think this is an aerial view of farmland when instead it pictures trays of diminutive collards, beets, lettuce, celeries, and herbs.

The Chef

"Localism is what drew me to Italian cuisine," says Executive Chef Melissa Close. History is repeated in the kitchen as well, where Close has expressed her fascination for classic Italian cooking since 2001. Chef Close directs all aspects of Palladio's kitchen: purchasing, menu creation, culinary technique, and final presentation of every plate. A native of Mobile, Alabama, Close worked in restaurants from age sixteen before attending the New England Culinary Institute. For more than ten years, beginning at Bottega Restaurant in Birmingham in the early 1990s, she has focused on regional Italian cuisine. She cooked at Rose Pistola in San Francisco until Craig Hartman named her sous-chef at the Cliff House in Colorado. Living by the tenet of "Don't get stagnant," she says, "I'm not an owner, I'm not a chef . . . I'm a cook." Handmade pastas, estate-grown mushrooms, and artisanal ingredients, the hallmarks of regional cuisine from Piemonte to Puglia, are

envisaged anew in central Virginia.

With such a wide swath of mid-Atlantic agriculture at its fingertips, the restaurant mirrors the "go-local" movement spreading across America, following the boom in farmers' markets, organic growers, and livestock raised with integrity. With more and more Virginia produce untouched by gratuitous pesticides and herbicides, it's not only easier now to maintain localism, "It's a shame if you don't," says Close. Listed on her menus are several of the state's best offerings: corn, cantaloupe, Swiss chard, collards, turnips, beet greens, cherries, peaches, figs, and strawberries that range from tangy to sweet.

House-cured duck prosciutto, cannelloni bean salad with red and yellow peppers, chives, and orange dressing, are a natural match for our crisp and fragrant Viognier Reserve

Yes, topflight restaurants now boast a fondness for regional ingredients, but how many chefs claim that the lion's share of herbs was grown but a few steps outside the kitchen door? In Palladio's case, the summer pesto begins in Barboursville's basil patch, and two retired growers

Bunet, a classic northern Italian chocolate custard, is part of our very traditional Italian cuisine.

Chef Melissa Close in action in the James Beard Foundation's kitchen in New York City on the occasion of a benefit wine dinner held on July 24, 2007.

continue to raise their impeccably-fresh vegetables and fruits just for Chef Close. This is paramount to Close. She describes the satisfaction of thumbing through seed catalogs and holding tomatoes still warm because they were picked that morning. "I'm a food purist," admits Close. "Olive oil, salt and pepper, and lamb grown twenty miles from here. . .".

Just as the philosophy of not over-manipulating ingredients is treated as law in Barboursville's vineyard management and viticulture, so it is in the restaurant, too. When the raw materials are so ripe and vibrant, sauces and preparations are minimal because they are meant to showcase flavor, not cover-up a lack of it. Instead, the elegant simplicity of Palladio's menu allows patrons to enjoy the bounty of Virginia and not merely the techniques of a chef.

"If you go to the Valtellina, there's buckwheat in the polenta," says Close. "South of Lake Como, it's just corn meal."

During the restaurant's annual January closing, Close and her sous-chef research some of Italy's finest restaurants, fueling Palladio's reputation for authenticity and innovation. Armed with weeks of observation steeped in tradition, she's "inspired to keep it that way" when returning home. This is how native dishes like "seared scallop with salsify purée" (oyster root) wend their way from Sicily to Virginia. On the other hand, Close is arguably at her best when tweaking tradition in the name of regionalism or inventiveness. For instance, her winter vegetable ratatouille with beets, turnips, and rutabagas mimics the summer classic, but with a definite nod to the seasons and Close's Southern roots.

Palladio's menu changes seasonally, but even regulars never get bored thanks to frequent wine dinners and monthly guest chef events when Close and her crew turn over their kitchen to renowned chefs from around the country. Moreover, an annual feast with the Virginia Opera – complete with Verdian arias – is both a culinary and cultural highlight. Yet, the most sought-after reservations year after year are "An Evening with Morels" in the spring, and the autumn "Truffle Dinner," each a spectacular marriage of Italian tradition and Virginian hospitality.

Below left: Tiramisù

Below right: Roasted peppers stuffed with tuna and capers.

Overleaf:
On occasion, Chef Close also creates more extravagant dishes such as scallop seviche in a parmesan shell with lemon zest and micro parsnips.

The Maître D'

Maître D' Alessandro Medici grew up in the province of Bergamo in Lombardia and attended the Professional School for Restaurateurs & Sommeliers in San Pellegrino Terme. Since 1990, his fine dining career has taken him from the Italian Alps to the Italian Riviera, from a private yacht on the Mediterranean to the Zonin household, before opening Palladio in 1999. Balancing elegant service with genuine country warmth, Medici and his genial manner, broad cravats, and expert palate are unforgettable facets of Palladio's charm. "The restaurant is my life," says Medici, "I've been here since day one. It's *cucina creativa* – Melissa respectfully uses local ingredients in a creative Italian fashion. People who've had the opportunity to dine in northern regions of Italy compare us to Michelin-starred restaurants and claim that Palladio is a corner of Italy . . . without the jet lag."

Note. the order of the terrasses below the garden wall is as follows.
the fig terras next to the wall. then
the walk terras.
the strawberry terras.
1st. terras of the vineyard & so on to the 17th.
the 18th. terras of the vineyard is occupied chiefly by trees.
the 19th. as Bailey's ally.

Mar. 25. S.W. vineyard. at S.W. end of 1st. terras planted 2. Malaga grape vines. Maine
at N.E. end. 1st. terras 12. black Hamburg grape vines.
2d. . . . 12. red do.
3d. . . . 10. white Frontignac.
4th. . . . 20. Chasselas.
5th. . . . 3. Muscadine
6th. . . . 11. Brickcoloured grapes.
7th. . . . 10. Black cluster grapes
} from Main. planted only in vacancies.

N.E. vineyard. beginning at S.W. end of it, & planting only in vacancies
1st. terras. 6. plants of Seralamanna grapes } 11. cuttings from them.
2d. . . . 15. cuttings of the same, or Piedmt. Malmesy
3d. . . . 13. Piedmont Malmesy. or Seralamanna
4th. . . . 1. Smyrna without seeds.
5th. . . . 7. Galettas.
6th. . . . 7. Queen's grapes.
7th. . . . 5. Great July grapes
8th. . . . 6. Tokay.
9th. . . . 13. Tokay.
10th. . . . 13 Trebbiano.
11th. . . . 17 Lachrima Christi.
12th. . . . 6. San Giovetto.
13th. . . . 15. Abrostine white
14th. . . . 21. do. red or Aleaticos
15th. . . . 15. Aleatico. or Abrostine red.
16th. . . . 13. Margiano.
17th. . . . 15. Mammole.

S.W. vineyard. N.E. end. 9th. terras 4. Tokays, same as 9th. of N.E. Vineyard.
10th. . . 6. Trebbianos. same as 10th. of N.E.
11th. . . 3. Lachrima Christi. same as 11th. of N.E.

Apr. 11. Nursery. begun in bed next the pales, on the lower side, where Genl. Jackson's peaches end to wit within 2. f. of the 4th. post from the S.E. corner.
No. 1. Quercus coccifera. Prickly Kermes oak. 3. cross rows.
2. Vitex Agnus castus. Chaste-tree. faux Poivrier. 9. rows
3. Cedrus Libani. Cedar of Lebanon. 2. rows.
4. Citisus Laburnum of the Alps. 2. rows.
5. Lavathera Albia. the shrub Marshmallow. 2. rows.
} seeds recd. from Doctr. Gouan at Montpelier.

Thomas Jefferson's ambitious list of grapevines to be planted at Monticello in 1807 shows varieties indigenous to growing regions as far-flung as Burgundy, Bordeaux, Tuscany, Alto Adige, and Asia Minor – 24 in all. Plainly, Jefferson anticipated that some varities would thrive better than others, allowing him to identify the wines likeliest to distinguish Virginia. In any event, there are no records to prove that this planting produced a harvest.

For additional reading:

Louis Alfano, *Filippo Mazzei – Godfather of the Declaration of Independence*, Location: http://www.geocities.com/circolomazzei/index.html

Adrienne Koch and William Peden, eds. *The Life and Selected Writings of Thomas Jefferson*, New York, NY: The Modern Library of New York, 1944.

Charles D. Lowery, *James Barbour: A Jeffersonian Republican*, Tuscaloosa, AL: University of Alabama Press, 1984.

Margherita Marchione, *Philip Mazzei: Jefferson's Zealous Whig*, Lanham, MD: University Press of America, 1994.

R. de Treville Lawrence, Sr., ed., *Jefferson and Wine*, The Plains, VA: Vinifera Wine Growers Association, 1973.

Chiles and Bernice Larson enjoy the charm and beauty of the estate from the balcony of The 1804 Inn.

Photograph Credits

The author and publisher wish to thank the following individuals, museums, institutions, and libraries for permitting the reproduction of works of art or photographs that they have taken or that are in their possession and for supplying the necessary photographs. All other photographs are by Chiles T. A. Larson.

Phil Audibert: 74; Barboursville Vineyards Archive, Michael Bailey: 44 and 79; Barboursville Vineyards Archive, Ben Fink: 69, 70, 83, 84, 85; 87 (both), 90, 91, and 96; Jon Golden: 8-9, 57, 75 (below), 77, and 88-89; The Historical Society of Pennsylvania, Ferdinand Julius Dreer Collection: 92; Independence National Historical Park: 24; Bernice Larson: back inside jacket flap; The Library of Virginia: x and 6; Massachusetts Historical Society: endsheets; The Montpelier Foundation: 19; Luca B. Paschina: ii, vi, 12, 25, 31, 37, 43, 56, 68, and 86; Réunion des Museés Nationaux/Art Resource, NY: 30; University of Virginia Alderman Library: 20-21; Casa Vinicola Zonin Archive: 45 (both), 46-47, 48, 54, 55 (all), and 58 (both); and Domenico Zonin: 66.

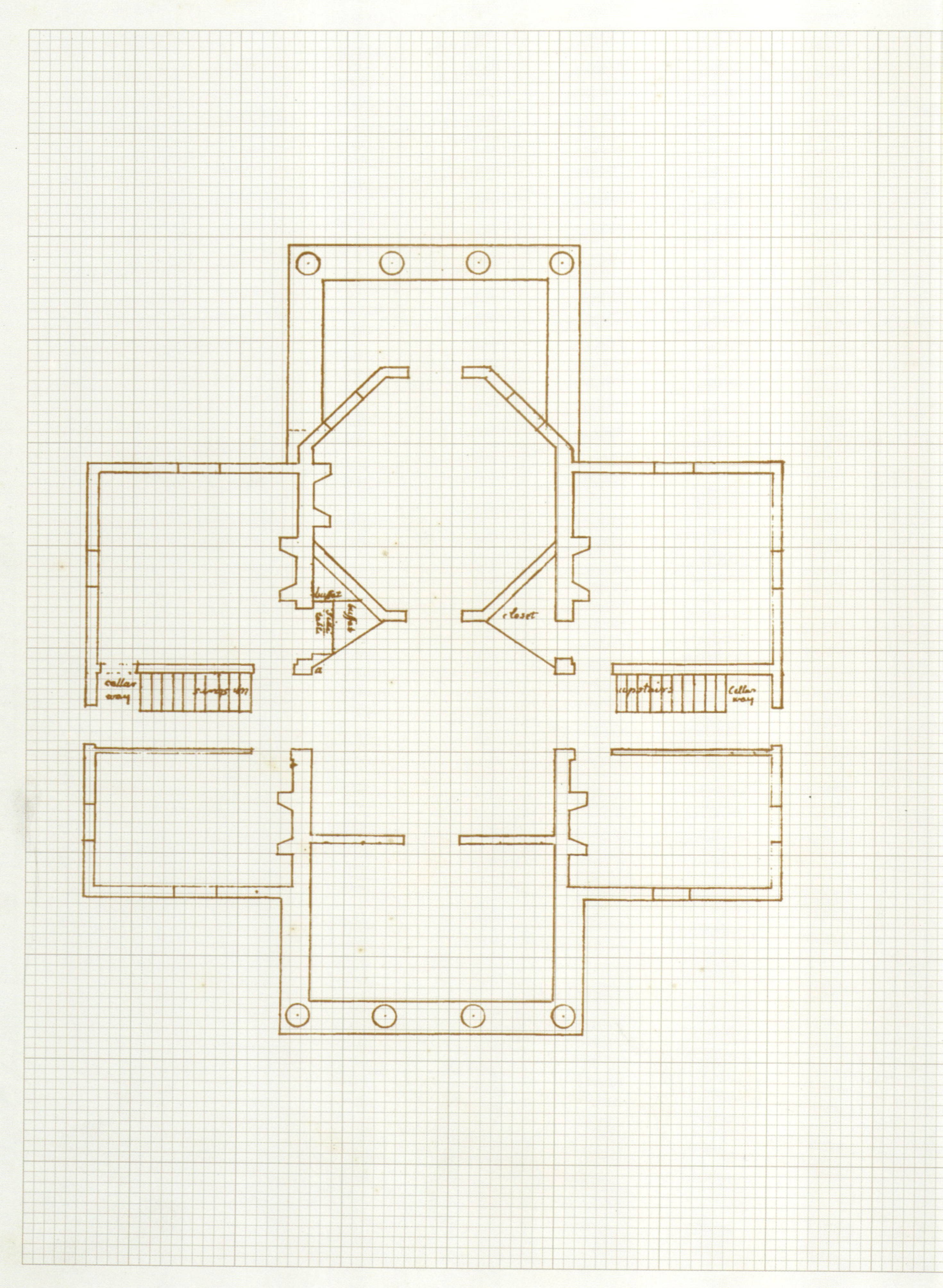
cellar way
buffet
buffet
a
closet
upstairs
Cellar way